A Giant Shield

A Study of the Atmosphere

Weather Books for Kids

Children's Earth Sciences Books

BABY PROFESSOR

EDUCATION KIDS

Speedy Publishing LLC
40 E. Main St. #1156
Newark, DE 19711
www.speedypublishing.com

Our Earth flies through space in an envelope of atmosphere. We breathe it, and it protects us in many ways. Read on and learn about the sky above us!

Our Atmosphere

Every time you breathe in, you take some of Earth's atmosphere into your body. It delivers the oxygen your cells need. Every time you breathe out, you get rid of carbon dioxide that your body cannot use. The atmosphere absorbs it and passes it on to plants, which use it with sunlight to make energy. The plants produce the oxygen that comes back to you. It's a really neat system!

What's In Air?

Our atmosphere is mainly air. So what is air? Air is a mix of gases, mainly oxygen, nitrogen and argon. Another element is water vapor. This can range from a tiny fraction of the atmosphere to as much as 5% of the volume of an air mass that is hot and humid, the sort of air mass that brings clouds and rain.

There are smaller amounts of gases like carbon dioxide, methane, ozone and nitrous oxide. People sometimes call these the "greenhouse gases". They help to trap the Earth's heat in the atmosphere, instead of letting it escape into space, the way the outer layer of a greenhouse keeps the warmer, moister air inside.

Pollen from a plant

There can also be dust, soot from pollution, traces of aerosol sprays, pollen from plants, and even foam from ocean waves that add into the mix. Volcanoes can suddenly add a contribution of ash that can travel far around the world and even change the Earth's climate. See the Baby Professor book What Happens Before and After Volcanoes Erupt? to learn more about volcanic ash.

Atmospheric Pressure

Atmospheric pressure is the pressure of all the atmosphere above a particular point. The base atmospheric pressure is at sea level, and its average around the world is the ISA, or International Standard Atmosphere. We measure atmospheric pressure in kilopascals or psi (pounds per square inch).

The further you move above sea level the lower the atmospheric pressure goes. You can notice this without leaving the ground! At sea level the average atmospheric pressure is 101.3 kilopascals, or 14.69 psi. At the top of Mount Everest, the world's highest mountain, the atmospheric pressure is only 33.7 kilopascals or 4.89 psi.

If you visit the Dead Sea in the Middle East, you are about 430 meters below sea level. There, atmospheric pressure is higher than it is at sea level: 106.7 kilopascals, or 15.48 psi.

What the Atmosphere Does

Our pleasant Earth moves through space, a very hostile area. Our atmosphere protects us from most of the dangerous stuff the universe throws our way.

Another way our atmosphere makes things easier for us is by smoothing out temperature changes. Without our atmosphere, Earth would be much hotter during the day and much colder at night. We can see this on the Moon, which has no atmosphere.

The daytime temperature on the Moon, where the Sun is shining on it, is about 100 degrees Celsius. But on the parts of the moon turned away from the Sun, the temperature drops to about -170 degrees Celsius.

Our atmosphere is thickest near the Earth's surface. As we move away from the ground, we move through different layers of the atmosphere. Let's check them out!

Troposphere

We'll start at ground level. Wherever you are on Earth, you are in the layer of atmosphere called the troposphere. The name comes from the Greek word for "mixing" and a lot of that happens in the troposphere. Warm, moist air rises from the land and the sea, and as it meets cooler air it forms clouds and weather patterns.

Rain and snow fall back down to earth, and the wind blows to stir up the dust on the Earth's surface and make the leaves in the trees move around. Sometimes the mixing of temperature, wind, air pressure, and other factors can make violent storms, like hurricanes and blizzards, that really mix things up!

Most of our weather happens in the troposphere, and even though it is only eleven miles thick, it holds about 80% of our air and almost all of the water vapor in the atmosphere. This means most of the weather we see and experience happens in the troposphere, close to the Earth's surface. Its temperature ranges from extremely hot, near the surface over deserts and cities, to well below freezing eleven miles up.

Stratosphere

The next layer up is the stratosphere, which reaches up about 30 miles above the Earth's surface. In this area is the ozone layer, a chemical layer that absorbs a lot of the energy of the Sun's ultraviolet rays. If there were no ozone layer, we could not survive because of the effects of the Sun's rays.

The atmospheric pressure at the top of the stratosphere is 1/1000 the atmospheric pressure at the Earth's surface. The stratosphere has almost no clouds and experiences very little in the way of weather.

Even though the stratosphere is further away from the Earth, its average temperature is warmer than that of the troposphere below it. That's because the ozone layer, absorbing energy from the Sun, adds heat to the layer. So the bottom of the stratosphere is about as cold as the coldest part of the troposphere, around -80 degrees Celsius, but the top of the stratosphere is around 0 degrees Celsius, the freezing point.

Mesosphere

As we move up through the mesosphere, the next layer, the temperature drops down again, as low as -180 degrees Celsius. The mesosphere reaches up to over 50 miles above the Earth's surface and is our meteor shield. Most meteors and other debris from outer space burn up from friction with the atmosphere in this layer.

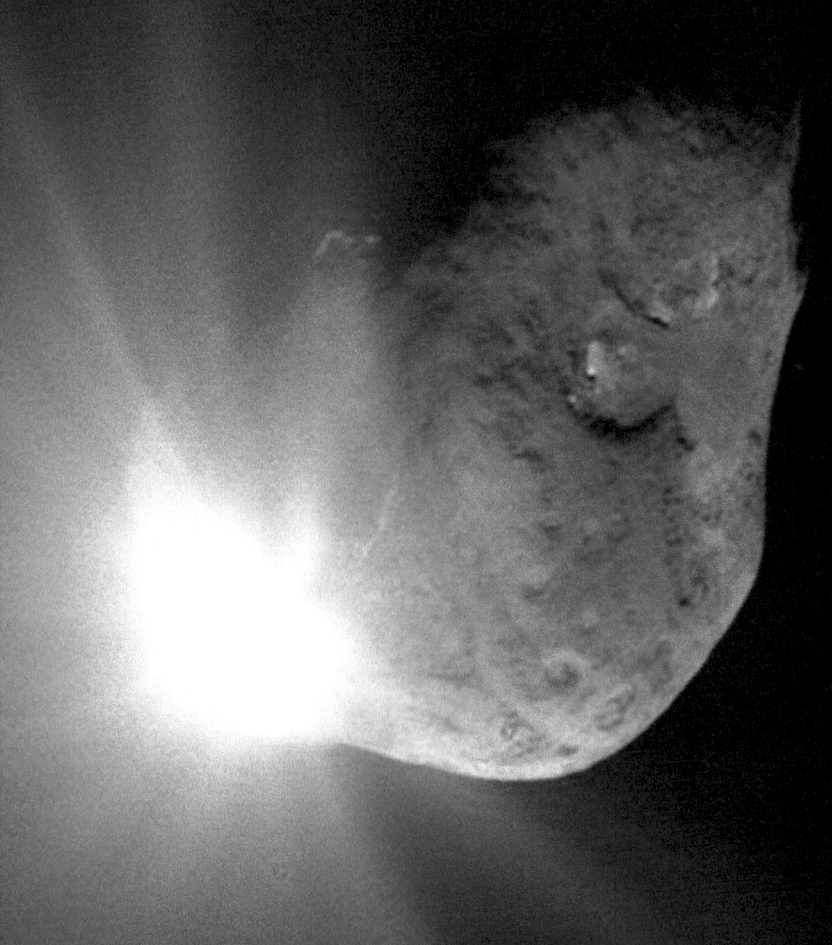
Meteorite image

We can see them as "shooting stars" on a clear night, especially at times of the year, like early August, when there is a major meteor shower. Meteorites, the small pieces of meteors that make it all the way to earth, are the fragments that survive from much larger chunks of rock and other materials that burned up in the mesosphere.

Ionosphere

The ionosphere extends almost 450 miles above the Earth's surface. The air molecules are so widely-spaced here that it is almost like the empty space between planets. Many earth satellites, and the International Space Station, orbit within the ionosphere.

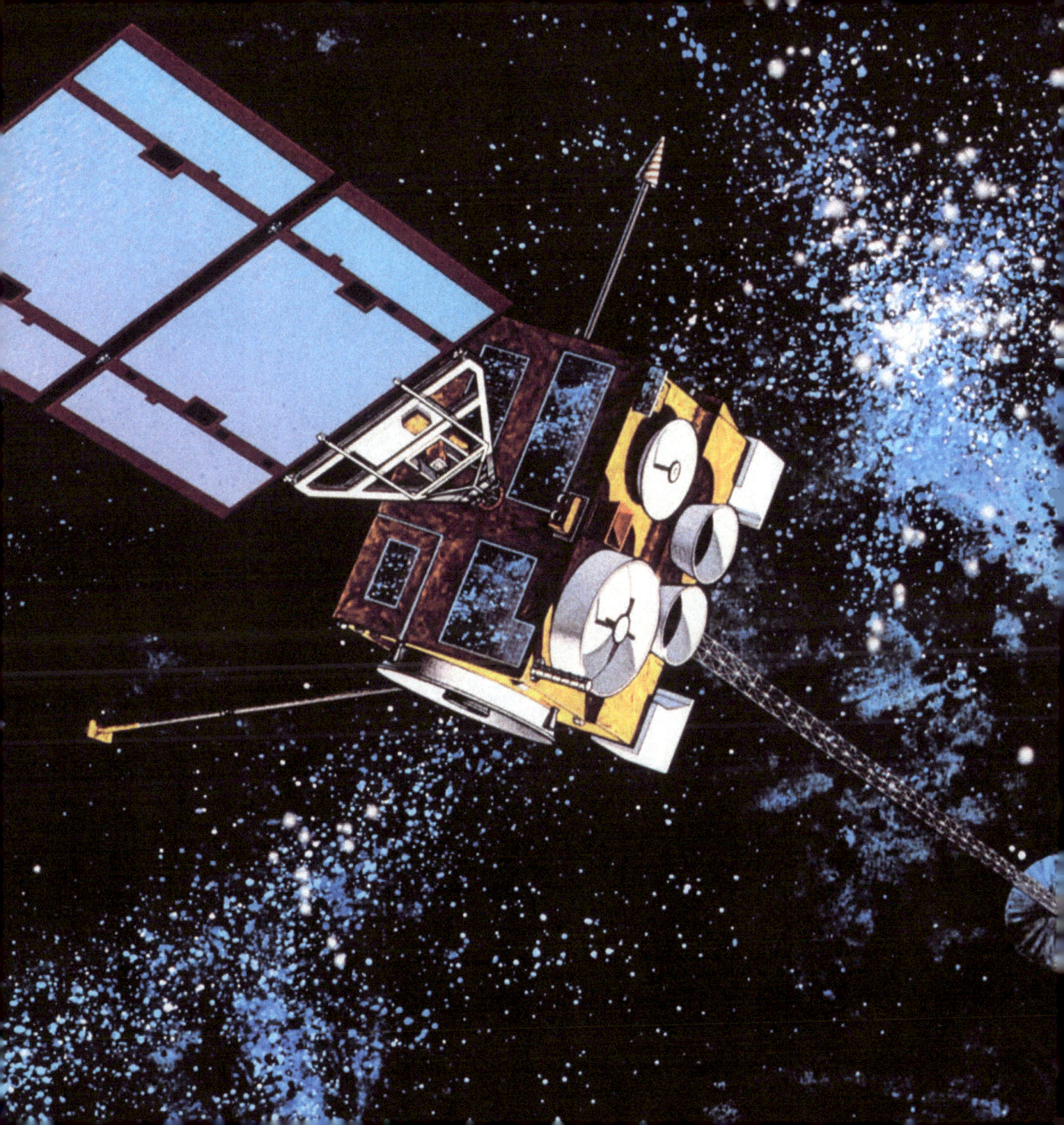

The name of this layer comes from the ions that solar energy and other energy from outer space create in this layer. These highly-charged particles make an electric layer around the Earth that can reflect radio waves. In the days before communications satellites that could relay signals, radio signals traveled farther than the visible horizon by "bouncing" off the ionosphere.

The ionosphere is also home to the Northern and Southern Lights or the auroras. These are colorful displays of charged particles that appear mainly over the North and South Poles. They can look like waving curtains or magical creatures, and they are the result of the energy in the solar wind and the ionosphere acting on each other.

Thermosphere

Another term for the ionosphere and the area of variable height above it is the thermosphere. Here the air is so thin that a single air molecule can travel a kilometer or more before it bumps into another one. This layer has no water vapor and so has no clouds.

Exosphere

The last layer is the exosphere. This is a filmy final edge to our atmosphere. When the solar wind is inactive, the exosphere can extend over six thousand miles from the Earth's surface. But in an active solar wind, the exosphere collapses inward until its outer edge is no more than 600 miles or so above the Earth. The molecules of the exosphere are widely separated, and they are mainly hydrogen and helium.

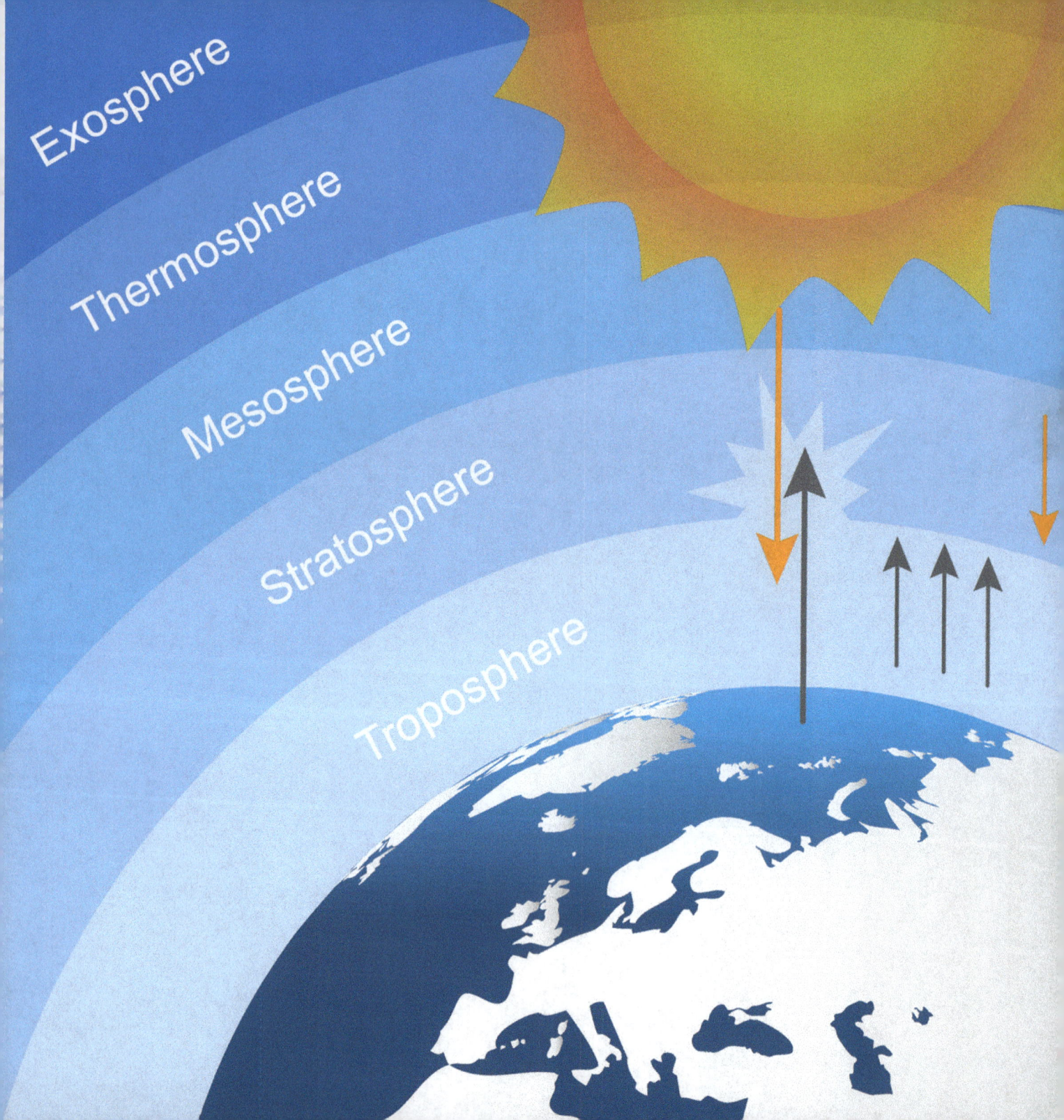

How the Atmosphere Developed

Earth's atmosphere has not always been as it is now. And we could not have breathed earlier forms of the atmosphere!

First Atmosphere

The first atmosphere around the developing Earth would have been mainly hydrogen, with methane, water vapor, hydrogen and ammonia. This was sort of like the atmosphere of the gas giant planets Jupiter and Saturn. This atmosphere mostly disappeared as the Sun took its final form.

THE EARTH'S ATMOSPHERE

Lorem ipsum dolor sit amet, consectetur adipiscing elit, sed do eiusmod tempor incididunt ut labore et dolore magna aliqua. Ut enim ad minim veniam, quis nostrud exercitation ullamco laboris nisi ut a liquip ex ea commodo consequat. Duis aute irure dolor in reprehenderit in voluptate velit esse cillum dolore eu fugiat nulla pariatur.

EXOSPHERE
>700-190.000 km

EXOBASE
>700-1000 km

THERMOSPHERE
80-700 km

Aurora Borealis

Sattelite

KARMAN LINE
100 km

Hubble

MESOSPHERE
50-80 km

Meteors

STRATOSPHERE
12-50 km

Fighter Jet

OZON LAYER
20-30 km

High Altitude Balloon

TROPOSPHERE
0-12 km

Baloon

Exosphere

Thermosphere

Mesosphere

Stratosphere

Troposphere

Earth

Second Atmosphere

A combination of volcanic action within Earth and asteroid bombardments from space generated a second atmosphere largely of carbon dioxide and nitrogen. A large part of this atmosphere converted into Earth's first water over 3.5 billion years ago. Soon after that life began to appear on Earth.

Third Atmosphere

Our current atmosphere is the third for this planet. About 2.5 billion years ago oxygen began to build up in the atmosphere. This put into place one of the essential elements for complex life, like the dinosaurs and you and me.

Over Our Heads and in Our Lungs

There is a lot going on in the atmosphere that is over our heads and in our lungs. Read other Baby Professor books, like A Kid's Guide to Weather Forecasting, to learn more.

Visit

BABY PROFESSOR
EDUCATION KIDS

www.BabyProfessorBooks.com
to download Free Baby Professor eBooks
and view our catalog of new and exciting
Children's Books

9 798869 411631